# Countries of the World

# Germany

by Michael Dahl

Reading Consultant:
Jonathan Clark, Ph.D.
Chairperson, Department of German and Norwegian
Concordia College

## Bridgestone Books
an Imprint of Capstone Press

Bridgestone Books are published by Capstone Press
818 North Willow Street, Mankato, Minnesota 56001
Copyright © 1997 by Capstone Press
All rights reserved
Printed in the United States of America

*Library of Congress Cataloging-in-Publication Data*
Dahl, Michael.
    Germany/by Michael Dahl.
    p. cm.--(Countries of the world)
    Includes bibliographical references and index.
    Summary: Discusses the history, landscape, people, and culture of Germany.
    ISBN 1-56065-523-2
    1. Germany--Juvenile literature. [1. Germany.] I. Title.
    II. Series: Countries of the world (Mankato, Minn.)
DD17.D34       1997
943--dc21
                              96-37747
                              CIP
                              AC

Photo credits
Beryl Goldberg, 12
Flag Research Center, 5 (left)
FPG, 6; Bruce Byers, 5 (right); Chuck Schmeiser, 8; Josef Beck, 10;
   Gleiter, 14; John Terence Turner, 16; Karin Reinhard, 18; Gebhardt, 20
International Stock/Mike Howell, cover

# Table of Contents

**Name:** Federal Republic of Germany

**Capital:** Berlin

**Population:** More than 81 million

**Language:** German

**Religions:** Protestant, Roman Catholic

**Size:** 137,735 square miles
(356,854 square kilometers)
*Germany is smaller than the U.S. state of Montana.*

**Crops:** Rye, barley, and wheat

# Maps

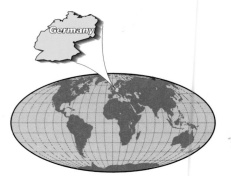

## Flag

Germany's flag has three stripes. A black stripe is on the top. A red stripe is in the middle. A gold stripe is on the bottom. A popular German saying about their flag is, "out of the darkness (black stripe), through blood (red stripe), and into the sunshine (gold stripe)."

## Currency

The deutsche (DOYTCH) Mark is the unit of currency in Germany. It takes 100 Pfennig (FEN-nig) to make one deutsche Mark.

*A Mark is like a U.S. dollar bill. A Pfennig is like a U.S. penny.*

# The Land of Germany

Germany is the third-largest country in Western Europe. Only France and Spain are larger than Germany. Germany is smaller than the U.S. state of Montana.

Germany is divided into 16 states. More than 81 million people live in these states. Many Germans live in cities.

Mountains and forests cover much of Germany. Southern Germany has many snow-covered mountains.

Northern Germany is very flat. It is by the seashore. Breezes from the North Sea keep the weather mild. Germans use much of their land to plant crops.

Germany was defeated in World War II (1939-1945). After that, Germany was divided into East Germany and West Germany. Now the people all belong to one country again.

**Forests and mountains cover much of Germany.**

# Going to School

Germans invented kindergarten. In Germany, kindergarten is not required. Most children choose to go anyway.

At six years old, German children start elementary school. Their parents give them a Schultüte (shul-TOO-te) on their first day. A Schultüte is a big paper cone. It is full of school supplies and special treats.

Students stay in school from 8 A.M. to 1 P.M. After school, children do their homework. Students go to elementary school for four years. Then they choose what school to attend.

They can choose training school. There they learn jobs that require special skills. Or they can go to a Gymnasium (Gim-NAH-zium). A Gymnasium is similar to a North American high school. Most students attend Gymnasium.

**Children take a Schultüte to school on their first day.**

# At Home

Hundreds of years ago, some Germans lived in castles. Many of these castles are still standing. Each year, millions of people tour the castles.

Today, most Germans live in apartments. People in the city fill their homes with plants. Almost every apartment and house has a small garden.

Germans wear clothes that are similar to those worn in North America. Once students had to wear uniforms to school. But now they can choose their own clothes.

People still wear old-style clothes for special events. Men and boys wear Lederhosen (LAY-der-hoh-zen). These are short pants made of leather. They wear felt hats with feathers, too. Women and girls wear bright dresses called Dirndl (DEERN-del).

**Many people visit the castles in Germany.**

11

# German Food

Germans eat their biggest meal in the afternoon. They usually eat different kinds of meat, potatoes, vegetables, and bread.

The evening meal does not have as much food. Germans might eat bread, cheese, fruit, or salad. Meals might also include beer or wine.

Different areas of Germany are known for special foods. In Bavaria (bah-VARE-ree-ah), people eat Schnitzel (SCHNIT-sal). Schnitzel is a specially prepared meat dish. People from Berlin like goose and thick pea soup. On the north coast, people eat eels mixed with fruit. Eels are snake-like fish.

Germans have more than 200 types of bread. They also have more than 100 kinds of sausage.

Germany has more than 100 kinds of sausage.

# Animals in Germany

Germany does not have many snakes, turtles, or lizards. Instead, weasels, beavers, and otters swim in the rivers. Deer, foxes, and wild boar roam through the forests. Boars are wild pigs.

The European Hedgehog is a favorite animal in Germany. Its picture is on greeting cards and writing paper. The hedgehog is also a popular stuffed animal.

Germans worry that pollution might hurt animals. Greens are people who want to improve the environment. They want to make Germany's land, air, and water clean.

People from around the world learn from the Greens. They learn how to stop pollution in their own countries.

**Foxes roam through Germany's forests.**

# German Sports

Germans enjoy many different sports. But soccer is the country's favorite sport. Most towns have a fussball (FOOS-bal) team. North Americans know fussball as soccer. Thousands of fans crowd into stadiums to watch fussball games.

Outdoor sports are popular in Germany. Every town has a swimming pool and a tennis court.

In the winter, many Germans ski in the mountains. Schools take students on trips to learn how to ski. In the summer, people hike and climb in the mountains.

Schools usually do not have sports teams. Many young people join sports clubs. The club is their team. That way they can play their favorite sport.

**Many people ski in Germany's mountains.**

# Berlin and the Autobahn

Most Germans live in cities. Many cities are built by rivers. This is because rivers were once the safest way to transport things.

Berlin is the capital of Germany. After World War II (1939-1945), it was divided by a wall. People were not allowed to cross to the other side of the wall. The wall was torn down in 1989.

Many people travel around Germany on electric trains. But Germans also enjoy driving. Special highways stretch between big cities.

These special highways are called the Autobahn (AH-toh-bahn). They have up to 10 lanes of cars. There is no speed limit on the Autobahn.

**There is no speed limit on the Autobahn.**

# German Holidays

German people celebrate many holidays. Most German people's favorite holiday is Christmas. Many years ago, Germans created the first Christmas tree.

German people also enjoy Saint Nicholas' Day. Saint Nicholas' Day is celebrated every December 6. It honors a Catholic saint who was famous for helping poor people.

Besides religious holidays, Germans have many festivals. Town festivals are popular. There are also festivals for horses, flowers, beer, music, and even sausages.

The most famous German festival is Oktoberfest. Every year many people gather in the city of Munich (MEW-nick). They eat, drink, and dance. The party lasts for 16 days.

Germany's newest holiday is held on October 3. It celebrates East and West Germany becoming one country again.

**Oktoberfest lasts for 16 days.**

# Hands On: Play Kegelin

Kegelin (KAY-guhln) is the German game of nine pins. It is similar to the American game of bowling. Nine pins was once the most popular game in early America.

## What You Need

Nine plastic soda bottles with caps
Sand
Soccer ball or softball
Paper and pencil

## What You Do

1. Fill the plastic soda bottles with sand.
2. Make sure the caps are on tight.
3. Arrange the bottles in a diamond shape.
4. Stand at least 15 feet (four and one-half meters) from the bottles.
5. Roll the ball at the bottles. Try to knock them all over.
6. You have two tries each time it is your turn.
7. Keep score on paper. Write down how many pins you knock down.
8. The winner is the person who knocks down the most pins.

X
XX
XXX
XX
X

## Learn to Speak German

| | | |
|---|---|---|
| **hello** | hallo | (HAHL-oh) |
| **good day** | guten Tag | (GOOT-un TAHG) |
| **good-bye** | auf wiedersehen | (owf VEE-der-zayn) |
| **no** | nein | (NINE) |
| **thank you** | danke | (DAHNK-uh) |
| **yes** | ja | (YAH) |
| **you are welcome** *and* **please** | bitte | (BIT-uh) |

## Words to Know

**Autobahn** (AH-toh-bahn)—special highways with no speed limit

**boar** (BORE)—a dangerous wild pig

**eel** (EEL)—a snake-like fish

**Greens** (GREENS)—people who want to make Germany's land, air, and water clean again

**Lederhosen** (LAY-der-hoh-zen)—short leather pants

**Schultüte** (shul-TOO-te)—a large paper cone filled with school supplies and special treats

23

## Read More

**Fairclough, Chris**. *Take a Trip to West Germany*. New York: Franklin Watts, 1981.

**Flint, David**. *Germany*. Austin, Tex.: Raintree Steck-Vaughn, 1994.

**Fuller Barbara**. *Germany*. New York: Marshall Cavendish, 1993.

**Haskins, Jim**. *Count Your Way through Germany*. Minneapolis: Carolrhoda Books, 1990.

## Useful Addresses and Internet Sites

**Embassy of the Federal Republic of Germany**
4645 Reservoir Road NW
Washington, DC  20007

**Pen Pal Planet**
P.O. Box 20111
Scranton, PA  18502

**Germany Information**
http://www.germany-info.org/

**Webfoot's Guide to Germany**
http://www.webfoot.com/travel/guides/germany/germany.html

## Index